DECISION-MAKING

IN THE WHITE HOUSE

THE OLIVE BRANCH OR THE ARROWS

DECISION-MAKING

IN THE WHITE HOUSE

THE OLIVE BRANCH OR THE ARROWS

THEODORE C. SORENSEN

FOREWORD BY JOHN F. KENNEDY

COLUMBIA UNIVERSITY PRESS

NEW YORK AND LONDON

Theodore C. Sorensen is Special Counsel to the President of the United States. He first joined the staff of the then Senator John F. Kennedy upon the latter's entry to the Senate in January, 1953. He was named one of the Ten Outstanding Young Men of the Year in 1961 by the United States Junior Chamber of Commerce.

COPYRIGHT © 1963 COLUMBIA UNIVERSITY PRESS

First printing 1963
Third printing 1964

LIBRARY OF CONGRESS CATALOG CARD NUMBER: 63-20465
MANUFACTURED IN THE UNITED STATES OF AMERICA

To My Mother and Father

THE GINO SPERANZA LECTURES

THIS book is based on the Gino Speranza Lectures for 1963, delivered at Columbia University on April 18 and May 9, 1963.

The Gino Speranza Lecture Fund was established in 1952 by a bequest of Mr. Speranza's wife, the late Florence Colgate Speranza, to provide annual lectures devoted to "American traditions and ideals, viewed from an historical viewpoint."

Contents

Foreword

THE American Presidency is a formidable, exposed, and somewhat mysterious institution. It is formidable because it represents the point of ultimate decision in the American political system. It is exposed because decision cannot take place in a vacuum: the Presidency is the center of the play of pressure, interest, and idea in the nation; and the presidential office is the vortex into which all the elements of national decision are irresistibly drawn. And it is mysterious because the essence of ultimate decision remains impenetrable to the observer —often, indeed, to the decider himself.

Yet, if the process of presidential decision is obscure, the necessity for it is all too plain. To govern, as wise men have said, is to choose. Lincoln observed that we cannot escape history. It is equally true that we cannot escape choice; and, for an American President, choice is charged with a peculiar and daunting responsibility for the safety and welfare of the nation. A President must choose among men, among measures, among methods. His choice helps determine the issues of his Presidency, their priority in the national life, and the mode and success of their execution. The heart of the Presidency is therefore informed, prudent, and resolute choice—and the secret of the presidential enterprise is to be found in an examination of the way presidential choices are made.

Many things have been written about the conditions of presidential decision. The President, for example, is rightly described as a man of extraordinary powers. Yet it is also true that he must wield these powers under extraordinary limitations—and it is these limitations which so often give the problem of choice its complexity and even poignancy. Lincoln, Franklin Roosevelt once remarked, "was a sad man because he couldn't get it all at once. And nobody can." Every President must endure a gap between what he would like and what is possible.

The loneliness of the President is another well-established truism of essays on the presidential process. It is only part of the story; for, during the rest of the time, no one in the country is more assailed by divergent advice and clamorous counsel. This advice and counsel, indeed, are essential to the process of decision; for they give the President not only needed information and ideas but a sense of the possibilities and the limitations of action. A wise President therefore gathers strength and insight from the nation. Still, in the end, he is alone. There stands the decision—and there stands the President. "I have accustomed myself to receive with respect the opinions of others," said Andrew Jackson, "but always take the responsibility of deciding for myself."

The author of this book has been an astute and sensitive collaborator in the presidential enterprise. Few writers have isolated the elements in presidential decision with such perception and precision. There will always be the dark and tangled stretches in the decision-making process—mysterious even to those who may be most intimately involved—but Mr. Sorensen, more than any recent American writer, has helped illuminate the scene with skill and judgment. He has been a participant, as well as an observer, of important decisions in difficult days. His careful observations have been made with skill and judgment and I am sure his work will become a permanent addition to the small shelf of indispensable books on the American Presidency.

The White House   JOHN F. KENNEDY
June, 1963

Introductory Remarks

Our lecturer this year has chosen the extraordinarily interesting and always timely topic of decision-making at the highest level—the White House.

One thing that has always impressed me in the course of such reading as I have been able to do has been that over the entire course of American history our Presidents have complained, sometimes privately in their diaries, sometimes privately to their friends, sometimes far more publicly, about the appalling responsibility of decision-making, a responsibility which they could not escape. We have had instances of Presidents who, aware that advisers always like to have their advice taken and are always unhappy if their advice is rejected or ignored, have tended to accept nearly all advice that has been offered to them—with disastrous consequences. And we have had some instances of Presidents who have generally tended to reject all advice, sometimes very good advice—with equally disastrous consequences. All of which I suppose indicates that there is no satisfactory generality one can possibly adopt to indicate when and why, how and under what circumstances, advice should be taken or rejected or, indeed, how this great burden of decision-making should be undertaken.

But I am impressed, as I am sure we all are, with the fact that in these days a new dimension has been added. In the past, there have been many eras in American history when Presidents could make decisions without worrying too much about what the consequences might be, because if the consequences were unhappy, the decision could be reversed and a new start made without any great harm. But today there is the new dimension. First, decision-making is made infinitely more difficult by the greater variety of contributory factors that have to be weighed before a decision is reached. This is a dimension that did not exist a generation ago. One shudders to think what this particular dimension may be a generation hence. And there is further, I should think, from what one can estimate from a distant view, the fact that decisions today are perhaps more irrevocable than in the past and tend to have far graver consequences.

So with these generalities, these clichés, in mind, you can see why we were enormously pleased when Mr. Sorensen agreed to accept our invitation to become the Speranza lecturer this year and to deal with various aspects or facets of the extraordinarily important, always significant, perhaps now-today-more-than-ever momentous problem affecting all of us. You know, of course, that Mr. Sorensen has been and is Special Counsel to President John F. Kennedy and that he was on the staff of Senator John F. Kennedy during his service in the United States Senate. Before that Mr. Sorensen was an attorney for the Federal Security Agency and received his undergraduate and legal schooling at the University of Nebraska.

With this invaluable experience in the turmoil of Washington life, and with this absorbing period of close association with the man who today is charged with the momentous burden of decision-making, Mr. Sorensen brings to us a rare expertise.

Columbia University   GRAYSON KIRK
in the City of New York
April 18, 1963

ONE

By Way of Introduction

TO speak of the American Presidency at Columbia in the very first lecture of my career is, I must confess, as bold a venture in the twentieth century as a schoolboy oration in Faneuil Hall on the subject of American liberty would have been in the nineteenth century. For it was at Columbia that Professor Woodrow Wilson delivered his memorable lecture redefining his views of the Presidency. It was there that Presidents Taft and Truman examined the office which they had occupied. There President Eisenhower presided over the campus before assuming the burdens of the White House. There distinguished scholars of the Presidency have served and now serve on the faculty, and both faculty and student body have produced over the years an extraordinary number of advisers to Presidents and presidential candidates—including, of course, the original Roosevelt study group that was given a name now loosely and often inaccurately applied to all presidential advisers: the "brain trust."

My choice of subject may also seem dubious in light of the countless number of works already published on the Presidency. Tomes have been written about presidential power—about the separation of powers, the delegation of powers, the sources and limits and now even the "ordeal" of power. There is no shortage of critiques on the American President's executive and administrative leadership—on the qualities required, the burdens imposed and the extent to which the office has risen or fallen (often influenced, I have noted, by the author's opinion of the man in office at the time). Historical studies tell us how many roles a President plays, how some have been strong and how some have been weak. And surely there is no dearth of material about my chief, the present incumbent—about his life, or his views, or his wife, or his youth—all told and retold, sometimes with more vividness than veracity, in journals both scholarly and sensational.

My lectures (and this book), therefore, were not directed at any of these subjects. Nor were they designed to play an even more popular game, that of analyzing the presidential machinery—assessing the role of the Cabinet or the National Security Council or the White House staff, stressing the need for new structures or new procedures or new ways to quicken the speed with which decisions are made, or specifying ways to lessen the gap from decision to action. There are already enough proposals to reorganize the Presidency to stretch from here to Utopia—and not all of them from academic circles. While there is some disagreement as to how successfully the Congress has organized itself, the Congress has not been timid about recommending wholesale reform of the Executive.

I do not question either the value or the relevance of all these studies. But to be preoccupied with form and structure—to ascribe to their reform and reorganization a capacity to end bad decisions—is too often to overlook the more dynamic and fluid forces on which presidential decisions are based.

Procedures do, of course, affect decisions. They especially affect which issues reach the top and which options are presented, and this may, in the last analysis, matter more than the final act of decision itself. But procedures and machinery do not—or at least they should not—dictate decisions, particularly in our highest political office. We may marvel at the speed and the efficiency with which an electronic computer can solve certain problems, but we would not vote for that computer to be President.

For "Governments," as Woodrow Wilson said in his lectures at Columbia, "are what politicians make them. . . . Government is not a body of blind forces [but] a body of men . . . not a machine but a living thing. It falls, not under the theory of the universe, but under the theory of organic life. It is accountable to Darwin, not to Newton."

In discussing the Presidency, therefore, I have taken my lead from the historic lectures delivered forty-two years ago by Judge Benjamin Cardozo on "The Nature of the Judicial Process." He did not focus his attention on the powers of judicial review and enforcement, or on the structure and rules of the American judiciary. He was concerned with how a judge decides a case, how his decision is shaped and limited. His lec-

4

tures were an attempt to examine, in his words, "all [the] ingredients enter[ed] in varying proportions into that strange compound . . . brewed daily in the caldron of the courts."

Can the same be done for the Presidency? Can we look beyond the organizational charts and ask: How does a President make up his mind? I refer not to psychoanalysis, but to the forces that shape his decisions. How does a President choose, for example, in a moment of crisis, between the olive branch of peace (clutched in the right talon of the eagle on his Seal) and the arrows of war (which are clutched in the left)? His alternatives, of course, are rarely that clear-cut—but, if not, why not? What limits the President's choice? What forces, what factors, what influences are blended in that final act of decision?

Obviously each President has his own style and his own standard for making decisions—and these may differ from day to day or from topic to topic, using one blend for foreign affairs, for example, and another for domestic. The man affects the office as the office affects the man.

Nor is decision-making something he neatly sets

aside for certain times or occasions. On the contrary, the President's entire existence is a continuous process of decision—including decisions not to decide and decisions not to take action—decisions on what to say, whom to see, what to sign, whom to name, and what to do, as Commander-in-Chief and diplomatic chief, as legislative leader and political leader, as a moral leader and a Free World leader, and in taking care that the laws be faithfully executed. Every policy announced is the sum of many decisions, each made in a different mold and manner.

I do not suggest, therefore, that there is any systematic formula of decision-making in the White House, any precise mixture of ingredients for one President to pass on to the next or even to use himself on successive occasions. I have no absolute tests to offer by which White House decisions can be judged, no new theories or concepts or terminology to describe this daily process. Indeed, the very frequency of the process increases the difficulty of subjecting it to logical analysis, of summarizing or synthesizing it in terms of some formal doctrine.

But I am convinced that whether a President is strong

or weak, whether he initiates or avoids decisions, whether he consults with his Cabinet or his Kitchen Cabinet, his brain trust or the "meat trust," the fundamental nature of the White House makes it inevitable that vital decisions, either many or few, will be made there, either by the President or with his consent, and that *the same basic forces and factors will repeatedly shape those decisions.*

The analysis which follows, therefore, is concerned, not with the influence of a President's decisions, but with what it is that influences them. It is my thesis that, however the institutions and the apparatus may be organized, these same basic influences are ever present—not by chance but by the nature of the office.

A President may ignore these forces or factors—he may even be unaware of them—but he cannot escape them. He may choose to decide in solitude, but he does not decide in a vacuum. As a painter mixes his colors, or a chef prepares his sauce, so he must mix these ingredients—omitting some if he wishes, or preferring others he likes, but mixing them nevertheless, in his own style and to his own taste, until the final product is fashioned.

BY WAY OF INTRODUCTION

Having participated briefly in this process, I offer my own observations of it. If some of my conclusions seem obvious, I include them only because of the dangers inherent in omitting what seems to be obvious.

TWO

The Setting for Decision

IN describing what forces might influence a President's decisions, I should first state with candor that these forces in the past have generally defied all description. The memoirs of some former Cabinet members would have us believe that they handed ready-made decisions to their President for his approval; yet their associates complain in *their* memoirs that the same Chief Executive was too proud to hear, much less to heed, good advice. My colleague Arthur Schlesinger, Jr., describes in fascinating fashion the maneuvers which preceded a decision by Franklin Delano Roosevelt, but then he adds: "Once the opportunity for decision came safely into his orbit, the actual process of deciding was involved and inscrutable." And Rexford Tugwell declared that Roosevelt "allowed no one to discover the governing principle" of his decisions.

President Truman wrote that "no one can know all the processes and stages of [a President's] thinking in making important decisions. Even those closest to him . . . never know all the reasons why he does certain things and why he comes to certain conclusions."

President Kennedy's analysis is still some years away from publication. Thus far he has referred simply to "the multiplicity of factors" that are involved in White House decisions.

But let us not be deterred in our quest by the characterization of this process as inscrutable or indescribable. On the contrary, if we can better understand why these decisions are like no others, if we can bear in mind what it is that comes to the White House for decision, and if we can review the component steps that go into these decisions, we will have some understanding of the setting in which they are made.

THE UNIQUENESS OF WHITE HOUSE DECISIONS

To begin with, White House decision-making is not a science but an art. It requires, not calculation, but judgment. There is no unit of measure which can weigh the substantive consequences of a decision against the political consequences, or judge the precise portions of public opinion and congressional pressure, or balance domestic against foreign, short-range against long-range, or private against public considerations.

Every decision a President makes involves uncertainty. Every decision involves risk. Almost every decision involves an element of prediction and at least latent disagreement with others. Bismarck believed that it was these "doubts and anxieties," not the burdens of the daily schedule, which were so wearing on a political official.

Elaborate guides to decision-making in private business or even in public administration are of little help in the White House. For the breadth and scope of presidential decisions cannot be matched in any large corporation or Cabinet department, or even in the halls of Congress. For the President alone is ultimately accountable for the lives of more than 2.5 million American servicemen, for the deeds of 2.5 million federal employees, and he alone is ultimately held accountable to 190 million citizens, to more than 40 foreign allies and, in a very real sense—as custodian of the nuclear trigger—to all men and to all mankind.

His decisions do not merely differ in degree from the decisions of others. No one else faces so many complex issues where the solutions are so remote, so dependent on the undependable, and so tinged with potential disaster. No one else, as Woodrow Wilson said, bears such multiple responsibilities in so many different and conflicting areas. No one else knows in advance that his decisions will be subject to such scrutiny, to such calumny, or to what Professor Neustadt calls such irreversibility.

In an age when not only this nation but also its chief adversary possess the capacity to inflict unacceptable disaster on another power in a matter of minutes, it is foolish to compare the role of the current President with that of any other man, including even his thirty-three predecessors. When President Kennedy, for example, reviewed with the nation his decision to resume nuclear testing in the atmosphere, every citizen could understand his stated desire to examine every alternative, to demand a thorough justification, and to consider all the consequences. But no one, not even those who served with him in high position, could truly know the weight of his responsibility or all the forces that induced his conclusion.

THE VOLUME OF WHITE HOUSE DECISIONS

Next, what is it that comes to the White House for decision? That, too, is a necessary part of the setting, but again there is no certain pattern. President Eisenhower rightly told President Kennedy: "There are no easy matters that will come to you as President. If they are easy, they will be settled at a lower level."

Some decisions are presented by the requirements of a President's calendar. He must, for example, send up a budget and presumably a legislative program at the start of each year, and these mean countless decisions. Some come to him by law, including bills to be signed or vetoed, nominations to be sent to the Senate, requests for a pardon or parole, and the review of certain quasi-judicial decisions.

But for the rest there are no set criteria. President Kennedy chooses to reach out and select key issues, to initiate deliberations, to anticipate crises. Other Presidents may prefer to decide only what cannot be decided below or only what others present.

In the White House, as elsewhere, "the squeaky wheel gets the grease"—and whenever a controversy looms large in the press or the Congress or the public mind, however small it may be in true perspective, it either lands on the President's desk or confronts him at a news conference. (The advisability of corporal punishment in the District of Columbia schools, for example, is not a major issue of state, but the predominance of that issue in the Washington press prior to one news conference caused President Kennedy to examine his own thoughts on the matter, and possibly his own youth.)

More importantly, when a President's own prestige is involved—or his own powers, posture, or reelection —or when an issue is too important for anyone else's word to be accepted, or too sensitive, or too unprecedented, or too likely to result in damage beyond repair —then a presidential decision is usually essential.

If I were to name the one quality which characterizes most issues likely to be brought to the President, I would say it was conflict—conflict between departments, between the views of various advisers, between the Administration and Congress, between the United States and another nation, or between groups within the country: labor versus management, or race versus race, or state versus nation.

Our society, after all, is founded on diversities and distinctions; free men thrive on inconsistent points of view; and our government is based on clashing checks and balances.

Presidents may even encourage such clashes within the government—by deliberately overlapping authority or inviting dissent, as Franklin D. Roosevelt did to make certain he heard the alternatives.

But conflict rarely needs a stimulus. The claims of domestic and foreign policy sooner or later collide. Congressional checks and balances are written into law. Public and political needs will often be incompatible. Competing policies or interest groups are sometimes equally deserving. And the heat that is generated by all of this friction will naturally rise to the top—to the presidential office.

Just as conflict will bring issues to the President, so

a lack of conflict may sometimes keep them from him even when he should be involved. For example: Had there been some disagreement between White House and State Department officials on the contents of a press statement on nuclear warheads in Canada, it would have been brought to the President's attention before it exploded in the headlines. To cite another case: proposed regulations on expense accounts, having been approved by everyone in Internal Revenue, were not presented to the President until they had been bitterly protested in public.

Of course, a President can so design his office and so delegate his authority as to keep certain or even most decisions away from him, but even then the decisions of others may require his intervention if he is to fulfill his constitutional obligation.

Some major issues do not regularly come before the President simply because they are low on his list of priorities and he chooses to rely on his appointed authorities.

Other issues are decided without presidential intervention because the Congress has placed plenary authority elsewhere, usually in the so-called independent agencies and commissions, where presidential persuasion may be operative but rarely presidential orders. Following the stock market decline of last summer, for example, many businessmen called upon the President to lower promptly the "margin" requirements for purchasing stock on credit. They did not realize that this decision was legally vested in the independent Federal Reserve Board.

On the other hand, a President's personal interests may draw to him decisions normally left for others. Roosevelt, for example, took a hand in deciding postage stamp designs. I have seen President Kennedy engrossed in a list of famous Indian chiefs, deciding on an appropriate name for a nuclear submarine. (Inasmuch as most of the chiefs had earned their fame by defying the armed might of the United States, it was not an easy decision. In fact, when he finally decided on Chief Red Cloud, the Navy protested that this name had undesirable foreign-policy implications.)

Time rules out many decisions. A President should not try to decide too few issues—but neither can he decide too many. Above all, he should decide what it is he need *not* decide at that time. During the October,

1962, Cuban crisis, the President charged his Cabinet and staff to avoid the presentation of those issues that could be safely delayed or settled among themselves. The postponement of some of these decisions, of course, required a more hurried handling in later weeks to meet budget or other deadlines, and this was not without difficulty, as the case of the Skybolt missile illustrates. There were other factors here in addition to the shortness of time, however, and surely no nonfeasance can be charged respecting the postponement of this issue by the Pentagon when war and peace were at stake.

THE MECHANICS OF WHITE HOUSE DECISIONS

Finally, what are the component steps in White House decision-making? It is not hard to state the ideal, but it is hard to state it with conviction. Theoretically it would be desirable to undertake, for each important decision, a series of carefully measured, carefully spaced steps, including ideally the following:

first: agreement on the facts;

second: agreement on the overall policy objective;

third: a precise definition of the problem;

fourth: a canvassing of all possible solutions, with all their shades and variations;

fifth: a list of all the possible consequences that would flow from each solution;

sixth: a recommendation and final choice of one alternative;

seventh: the communication of that selection; and

eighth: provision for its execution.

In these ideal and mechanical terms, White House decision-making sounds easy, if somewhat elaborate. It is simply the interaction of desire and fact—simply a determination of what the national interest requires in a given situation. But unfortunately it is neither mechanical nor easy; nor, it should be added, is the amount of care and thought devoted to a particular decision necessarily proportionate to the formality and regularity of the decision-making process.

For the ideal case is the exception. Each step cannot be taken in order. The facts may be in doubt or dispute. Several policies, all good, may conflict. Several means, all bad, may be all that are open. Value judgments may differ. Stated goals may be imprecise. There may be many interpretations of what is right, what is possible, and what is in the national interest. A President's decision may vary according to how the question is formulated and even by who presents it. All his available choices may be difficult mixtures of both good and evil.

For every course he examines, there will always be some opposition in the country, in the Congress, and even among his advisers. There will always be one adviser to say, after the fashion of certain columnists and commentators, that "on the one hand" consider this but "on the other hand" think of that. Idealists on his staff will rule out expediency. Realists will disregard morality. Some will counsel speed; others will counsel delay—yet even delay will constitute a decision.

As each President nears a final answer, he realizes that this choice is only the beginning. For each new decision sets a precedent, begetting new decisions, foreclosing others, and causing reactions which require counteraction. Roosevelt, according to Madam Perkins, "rarely got himself sewed tight to a program from which there was no turning back." And President Kennedy, aware of the enormous hazards in the confrontation with the Soviets over Cuba in October, 1962, made certain that his first move did not close out either all his options or all of theirs.

But too often a President finds that events or the decisions of others have limited his freedom of maneuver—that, as he makes a choice, that door closes behind him. And he knows that, once that door is closed, it may never open again—and he may then find himself in a one-way tunnel, or in a baffling maze, or descending a slippery slope. He cannot count on turning back —yet he cannot see his way ahead. He knows that if he is to act, some eggs must be broken to make the omelet, as the old saying goes. But he also knows that an omelet cannot lay any more eggs.

THREE

The Outer Limits of Decision

ALL this has been by way of introduction and background, important to an understanding of White House decision-making but revealing little of the process itself. The question still arises: what forces or factors converge to shape these decisions? What recurring threads are woven together in a President's final choice?

It is my view that three fundamental kinds of forces influence most White House decisions, to be discussed in terms of presidential advisers, presidential politics, and the presidential perspective. In these three terms of reference, I shall undertake to group all of the elements which mold presidential choices. But before I can discuss these three forces, let me first turn to the limits within which these forces operate—the frame on which the cloth is woven.

For no President is free to go as far or as fast as his

advisers, his politics, and his perspective may direct him. His decisions—and their advice—are set within at least five ever-present limitations. He is free to choose only: 1) within the limits of permissibility; 2) within the limits of available resources; 3) within the limits of available time; 4) within the limits of previous commitments; and 5) within the limits of available information.

Some of these limits operate directly on the President; others shape the choices that come before him. In logical terms, it may be difficult to differentiate between these "limits" and the "influences" to be described later on. They may on occasion be interchangeable or even indistinguishable.

But whatever the difficulties of semantic classification, I believe these five limitations are there. They may often be stretched. They may sometimes be absent. But they cannot be broken or ignored by a President on too many occasions without his suffering the consequences.

I would guess that Woodrow Wilson, for example, upon completion of his second term—his dreams shattered as well as his health, his proposals rejected as well as his party—regarded the presidential office with a somewhat different view than he had expressed in his Columbia University Lecture some fourteen years before. "The President is at liberty," he had then declared, "both in law and conscience, to be as big a man as he can. . . . His office is anything he has the sagacity and force to make it. . . . His capacity will set the limit."

LIMITS OF PERMISSIBILITY

Wilson, and all who preceded and succeeded him, found that there are other limits. There are, first of all, limits of permissibility. In a government of laws, a President is not free to ignore the Constitution he is sworn to uphold, the statutes he is obliged to enforce, the decisions of our Courts, and the rights of citizens and states. And to this body of law, as the world grows smaller, must be added international law, which cannot be dismissed as quickly as some claim.

For example: had the Organization of American States failed in October, 1962, to provide the necessary two-thirds vote authorizing a Cuban quarantine, the Soviets and possibly others might have been emboldened to challenge the legality of our action, creating confusion and irresolution in the Western camp and giving rise to all kinds of cargo insurance and admiralty questions that this nation would not enjoy untangling.

Permissibility as a limit to decision-making, however, is not a matter of law alone. A decision in foreign affairs almost always depends on its acceptance by other nations, and, as President Kennedy once ruefully remarked, the leaders of every nation seem to believe that the United States can change the minds and course of all nations but their own. A decision in domestic affairs (and often in foreign affairs, as in the case of Yugoslav trade) may depend on its being accepted, or its not being reversed, by the Congress—for the President under our system is not empowered to remake the nation in his own image.

Surprisingly enough, a President's decision in either domestic or foreign affairs may also depend upon its acceptance within the Executive branch itself—on the President's ability to gain acceptance for his point of view over dissent, inertia, incompetence, or impotence among his own appointees and policy officials as well as the permanent bureaucracy. Few outsiders understand this—they view the Executive branch as a monolith, where the President's every word is a command and all lines of authority run to him. But in truth there are checks and balances within the departments and agencies—and I can recall more than one occasion when it was necessary for the President to convince his own appointees before they could undertake to convince the Congress, the Soviets, or some other party.

Nor is it enough that a decision be acceptable. It must also be workable. It must be enforceable. It must be possible. The President is not omnipotent. Choices within his control may be altered by events beyond his control. Revolutions, assassinations, elections, and disasters daily change the face of the globe. A decision to maintain a nuclear test moratorium may be shattered by a Soviet resumption. A decision to use only federal marshals to protect a Negro student in Mississippi may be reversed by the violence of a mob. A decision to lower the deficit by withholding taxes on dividends may be rejected by the Congress.

In the minds of the public and the press, as Philip Jessup has said, "impossibility is sometimes confused

with incompetence or indecision." In the summer of
1962, for example, the pressures on the President to request a quick tax cut before the election were very large.
His delay was attributed by some to indecision. Yet in
the absence of economic evidence sufficiently alarming
to overcome key congressional objections—evidence
which was never forthcoming—such a request would
have been only an exercise in futility, and possibly a
harmful one at that.

There is no clear standard of feasibility. It may depend on the President's prestige at the moment of decision, as was notably true in the first hundred days
of Franklin D. Roosevelt. It can be affected by an unexpected turn of events—such as occurred when the
thalidomide tragedy increased the acceptability of drug
reform. What *is* clear is that a President's authority is
not as great as his responsibility—and that what is desirable is always limited by what is possible or permissible.

LIMITS OF AVAILABLE RESOURCES

Second, there are limits of available resources. It is a
law of life that every gain incurs a cost—and the most
efficient decision, therefore, is theoretically the one

which produces the greatest margin of gain over cost. But, in government and politics, gains are hard to measure and costs are hard to predict. One gain may breed another, while the cost of failure may plummet out of control.

A President's resources are limited, not only in terms of money, but in terms of manpower, time, credibility, patronage, and all the other tools at his command. If he appoints a distinguished Secretary of Labor to the Supreme Court, he loses him from his Cabinet. If he allocates a billion dollars of his budget to education, it cannot be used for public works. If large numbers of scientists are recruited for a moon-shot, they are not available for other needs.

Only a limited number of commodities can be reserved from meaningful trade negotiations. Only a limited number of times can key members of Congress or leaders of the alliance be approached with special requests. Only a limited number of televised appeals can be made to the nation without the danger of diminishing returns.

Any President, in short, must always be setting priorities and measuring costs. The official most often likely to loom largest in his thinking when he makes a key decision is not the Secretary of State or the Secretary of Defense but the Director of the Budget.

LIMITS OF AVAILABLE TIME

Third, there are limits of available time. There is "a time for every matter under heaven," the Scriptures say, "a time to keep silence and a time to speak . . . a time for war and a time for peace." Certainly time is of the essence in a presidential decision. There is a time to act and a time to wait. By not acting too soon, the President may find that the problem dissolves or resolves itself, that the facts are different from what he thought, or that the state of the nation has changed. By not waiting too long, he may make the most of the mood of the moment, or retain that element of surprise which is so often essential to military and other maneuvers.

Franklin D. Roosevelt was reputed to be a master of political timing. Mrs. Roosevelt spoke of his "enormous patience," his ability to "wait for exactly the right moment to act." "Though he enjoyed giving the impression of snap decisions," writes Schlesinger, he

29

"actually made few," and had, in fact, a "weakness for postponement"—waiting until the situation had crystallized, until conflicts between competing forces were resolved, until public opinion was united.

Postponement often can be a weakness. Secrecy in government is sometimes necessary, but it is rarely permanent; and the topics of decisions long postponed are likely to be revealed before the decision is taken. The desire for more argument or more facts is always pressing, but overly prolonged fact-finding and debate may produce answers to questions which no longer exist. In the White House, the future rapidly becomes the past, and delay is itself a decision.

Yet most presidential decisions are too far-reaching and too irrevocable to be taken in haste, when the facts are uncertain, when the choices are unclear, or when the long-range consequences are not as discernible as the immediate reactions and results. President Kennedy has said, with respect to the Cuban crisis: "If we had had to act in the first twenty-four hours, I don't think . . . we would have chosen as prudently as we finally did."

Some observers have argued that the President should

have been told of that ominous missile discovery the night the first evidence came in. Yet there was no action to be taken that night of a retaliatory or investigative nature, nor any reason to believe that his options would be different in the morning, when the actual presentation could be made. The departure of dinner guests to sudden midnight meetings at the White House might have served only to spread the alarm, and untroubled presidential sleep—an all too rare and therefore carefully guarded commodity—was a better preparation for the days ahead than a fruitless night of discussion.

As the exhaustive and exhausting deliberations of that long October week went forward, however, the limits of time did become more pressing. For all of us knew that, once the missile sites under construction became operational, and capable of responding to any apparent threat or command with a nuclear volley, the President's options would be drastically changed. And all of us knew that, once the Soviets learned of our information and planning, our prospects for surprise and initiative would be greatly lessened. The President, therefore, could not wait for unanimity among all his advisers or for a special congressional session. The lonely decision was his—and he made it in good time.

Under any President, life in the White House is a series of deadlines: a new measure to be proposed before the old law expires, an executive order to be issued while the Congress is out of session, a dispute to be resolved before the President's next press conference. At times, the President will deliberately impose a deadline as a means of limiting debate. When the time and topic of a televised speech have been announced, for example, departments concerned with that subject, however laggard they may have been up to then, will make certain that their views are crystallized and forcefully presented.

LIMITS OF PREVIOUS COMMITMENTS

Fourth, there are limits of previous commitments, including the commitments or principles of the nation or party, the commitments or precedents of an earlier President, the commitments or decisions of a subordinate official, and the statements of the President himself.

Of all these, party platforms and campaign promises

are often the least confining, for they are usually worded by both parties with sufficient art to permit some elasticity, if not evasion.

On the other hand, even though they come from different political parties, a President will find that his predecessor's guarantee of some little nation's military security, for example, is not easily reversed, no matter how greatly the problem has changed. Similarly, the actions of that predecessor may set a precedent which the nation assumes will be followed—as, for example, in the use of federal troops to enforce court-ordered desegregation, or the release of detailed information on the President's physical ailments. President Kennedy's successor, regardless of party, will find it difficult to reverse the nation's present course in space or in Latin America. Whatever the merits of these various decisions, it is clear that no President starts out with a clean slate before him.

And even after he is in office, he cannot easily reverse a promise made by a subordinate—by an ambassador on foreign assistance, for example, or on the recognition of a new government—if that man's stature in the host country is to continue to be respected.

But the clearest limitations of all are those imposed

by a President's own decisions. He need not make a fetish of consistency but he must avoid confusion or the appearance of deception. He will in most cases, therefore, adopt his own policies as precedents and consider his own statements as binding, whether they were contained in an informal answer to a press conference question or in a formal document of state. If the President solemnly promises to submit a balanced budget—or to reduce the outflow of gold—or to curb civilian appropriations—the country, the Congress, and the Executive branch will all assume that such pledges were not lightly made and must not be lightly taken; and the weight of those words will narrow many subsequent presidential choices.

To refer once again to this nation's response to the presence of Soviet missiles in Cuba, this decision was not wholly developed during the seven days preceding its announcement. President Kennedy, on the morning of the first of those seven days, sent for copies of all his earlier statements on Cuba—on the presence of offensive, as distinguished from defensive, weapons—on threats to our vital interests—and on our armed intervention in that island. These earlier decisions made it unlikely that he would respond to the October crisis by doing nothing and unlikely that his first step would be an invasion.

Here, too, the nation's basic commitment to tradition and principle was involved. An air strike on military installations in Cuba, without any advance warning, was rejected as a "Pearl Harbor in reverse"—and no one could devise a form of advance warning (other than the quarantine itself, which was a type of warning) that would not leave this nation vulnerable to either endless discussion and delay (while work on the missiles went forward) or to a harsh indictment in the opinion and history of the world.

Similarly, in the summer of 1961, our diplomatic and military responses to each aggravation in West Berlin were kept consistent with general allied policy in the area. And the fiscal questions this crisis posed are an example of two prior commitments in conflict. A tax cut at that time, while it might have strengthened the economy at a crucial moment, could not be included in an emergency program for increasing burdens and effort; while a tax increase, though it might have helped pay for rising defense costs, would have been incompatible with the President's pledge on the nation's economic recovery. "The special train," Dr. Jessup has said, "must run on the same tracks which carry the regularly scheduled traffic."

Consistency in decision, let me make clear, is not simply a matter of a President's "image." Even in our rapidly evolving society, even under a progressive administration, innovation is more difficult than continuation. For machinery must be rearranged. The public—or the Congress—or the allies—must be persuaded. New costs must be incurred, and old expenditures may be wasted. Having once made a decision— to build an expensive weapons system, or to assist in some nation's defense, or to send a man to the moon —a reversal of that decision is deterred in part by the prospects of losing the investment already made.

LIMITS OF AVAILABLE INFORMATION

Fifth, there are the limits of available information. Implicit in this limit is the President's need to make certain that as much information as possible is available. Reliance on official channels only has never proven to be wise. For there will always be subordinates who are willing to tell a President only what they want him to hear, or, what is even worse, only what they think he wants to hear.

Franklin D. Roosevelt made a systematic effort to supplement the official sources of information, not limiting his search to the somewhat rarified and often provincial atmosphere of Washington, D.C. Similarly, President Kennedy, although he is careful to rely primarily on the responsible officers involved when a final decision is to be taken, seeks independent information from a vast variety of unofficial sources: newspapers, magazines, books, radio, television, visitors, friends, politicians, pollsters, the spokesmen for private organizations, and a sampling of White House mail.

But add any or all of these to the inevitable and inexorable tides of official memoranda, reports, cables, intelligence briefings, analyses, and other government documents, and the occupant of the White House becomes subject to drowning in paper. All Presidents, at least in modern times, have complained about their reading pile, and few have been able to cope with it.

There is a temptation, consequently, to cut out all that is unpleasant, yet rational decisions require an understanding of opposed positions. There is a temptation to require more screening of information, with only the most salient facts filtering through on one-page memoranda. But only if he immerses himself in the problem will a President know what questions he must ask if he is to find the answers he must give. While he cannot permit himself to be submerged in detail, he cannot afford to know so little as to shut out perspective and new inspiration.

It is commonly said that our Presidents need more time set aside to do nothing but think. Yet presumably we elect a man who is thinking all the time, who is thinking when reading or listening or conferring. Our real concern should be that the President has all the facts he needs to make certain he is thinking with profit. The "lonely isolation" of the Presidency refers to the solitude of his responsibility—not to insulating him from all the pressures, paper work, and discussions which are essential to his perspective.

To make informed decisions, the President must be at home with a staggering range of information—about history, economics, politics and personalities in fifty states and now in a hundred or more countries.

He must know all about the ratio of cotton acreage to prices, of inventory accumulations to employment, of corporate investment to earnings, of selected steel prices to the economy, and of the biological effects of fall-out to the effects of natural radiation. He must cope with issues for which no previous experience on earth can equip him. For the essence of decision is choice; and, to choose, it is first necessary to know.

No President, of course, pays attention to all the information he receives, nor can he possibly remember it all. What he actually considers and retains may well be the key to what he decides, and these in turn may depend on his confidence in the source and on the manner in which the facts are presented. He is certain to regard some officials and periodicals with more respect than others. He is certain to find himself able to communicate more easily with some staff members than with others. He is certain to find that some reports or briefing books have a higher reliability than others, that some can be skimmed and some even skipped.

The primary problem of presidential information, however, is usually not an abundance of reliable data but a shortage, especially in foreign affairs. The apparatus and operations of modern intelligence systems can obtain and assemble great quantities of heretofore unreachable facts, but they cannot predict the future. And it is the future which most often must be gauged.

In these last two years, for example, the President has had to judge whether this nation's resumption of nuclear tests would increase or diminish the prospects for a test ban treaty, whether new military assistance to the Congo would assure its pacification or bring it back into the Cold War, whether our quarantine around the island of Cuba would lead to Soviet submarine warfare, to a Berlin blockade, or to Soviet ships turning back.

Domestic decisions also involve uncertainty: whether a presidential appeal for his health insurance program would diminish or stiffen the opposition, whether presidential criticism of a union or industry which is threatening industrial peace or price stability would bring a reconsideration or merely an angry rebuff, whether a presidential order banning discrimination in federal housing would achieve its objectives or simply cause a shifting of financing to other sources or a weakening of the housing market, whether the state and local authorities in Oxford, Mississippi, could keep order without federal troops or had never intended to do so.

These are the kinds of facts a President would like to know but cannot know on the domestic scene, where one miscalculation can endanger his entire program. But the gaps in his information are even greater on the world scene—and there one miscalculation can endanger the nation, or even life as we know it on this planet.

Yet decisions must be made. Despite the gaps in his information, despite the strictures of his previous pledges, despite the crowding of his schedule and the shortage of waking hours, despite the narrowness of his available resources and the restrictions on his permissible options—despite all these limitations, the President must, nevertheless, make decisions every day on courses for the nation that may decide its success or survival.

Few Presidents, therefore, I am certain, could survive themselves unless they had the capacity to say, as Franklin D. Roosevelt reportedly said to a friend:

"At night, when I lay my head on my pillow . . . and I think of the things that have come before me during the day, and the decisions I have made, I say to myself —well, I have done the best I could—and I turn over and go to sleep."

President Harding, on the other hand, was one of those who did not survive; and he is reported to have burst out to a friend: "I listen to one side and they seem right, and then . . . I talk to the other side and they seem just as right, and there I am where I started . . . God, what a job!"

What a job it is, indeed. As discussed in the pages that follow, the President may seek advice from the Congress, from the Cabinet, or from his personal advisers. He may seek the views of the press, the parties and the public. But however numerous his counsellors, in that final moment of truth there can be no "multitudes, multitudes" in the "valley of decision." There can be only one lonely man—the President of the United States.

FOUR

Presidential Politics

WE can turn now to the major forces or sources of influence which shape the presidential decision itself, grouped under three frames of reference: presidential politics, presidential advisers, and the presidential perspective. (All of these classifications are arbitrary and imprecise, and another observer with equal logic and accuracy might well have listed twenty-three or indeed forty-three subdivisions.)

Some purists—if not realists—may blush at the fact that politics heads the list. But we are discussing our prime political office and the nation's prime politician, a man who has been chosen by his party as well as the people. Some Presidents may assert that they are "above politics," yet politics, in its truest and broadest sense, still colors their every decision (including the decision to appear nonpolitical). Some issues have been traditionally deemed to be outside of politics, but considerations of public and congressional support still affect their disposition.

There is nothing dishonorable about the influence of politics on White House decisions. In a nation governed by the consent of the governed, it is both honorable and indispensable. While limitations of responsibility and accuracy should always be present, to say that we should remove such issues as Berlin or Red China from politics is to say they should be removed from public accountability and scrutiny. To charge that a President is politically motivated when he advocates a tax cut or a strong civil rights measure is simply to charge that he is doing what every elected official is elected to do.

Politics pervades the White House without seeming to prevail. It is not a role for which the President sets apart certain hours. It is rarely the sole subject of a formal presidential meeting. It is instead an ever-present influence—counterbalancing the unrealistic, checking the unreasonable, sometimes preventing the desirable, but always testing what is acceptable.

44

PUBLIC OPINION

But democratic government is not a popularity contest; and no President is obliged to abide by the dictates of public opinion. Our political idealism may be filled with assumptions of human virtue and wisdom, but our political history is filled with examples of human weakness and error.

Public opinion is often erratic, inconsistent, arbitrary, and unreasonable—with a "compulsion to make mistakes," as Walter Lippmann put it. It rarely considers the needs of the next generation or the history of the last. It is frequently hampered by myths and misinformation, by stereotypes and shibboleths, and by an innate resistance to innovation. It is usually slow to form, promiscuous and pervidious in its affection, and always difficult to distinguish. For it rarely speaks in one loud, clear, united voice.

A President, therefore, must remember that public opinion and the public interest do not always agree. The value to this nation of a foreign aid program, for example, is not determined by its popularity. Last year's trade expansion bill could not have awaited a spontaneous public demand. Voter enthusiasm for our space effort is high after each flight of a Soviet or American astronaut, but in between flights new doubts and complaints will emerge. And almost any pollster in any state will find that most voters want higher federal expenditures in their areas of interest, lower expenditures elsewhere, and a balanced budget always.

No President could simply respond to these pressures. He has a responsibility to lead public opinion as well as respect it—to shape it, to inform it, to woo it, and win it. It can be his sword as well as his compass. An aroused public opinion was more effective in 1962, for example, in helping create a climate favorable to the rescission of steel prices, than any statutory tool. President Kennedy's televised explanations of his decisions on Berlin, nuclear testing, and the Cuban quarantine achieved on each occasion a new national consensus that discouraged any adversary's hopes for disunity.

But arousing public opinion is a delicate task. President Kennedy's plea for fall-out shelters in his 1961 discussion of Berlin ended the prevailing national apathy on civil defense, but it also unleashed an emotional response which grew to near-hysterical proportions (before it receded once again to near-apathy). His warnings on the presence of Soviet missiles in Cuba had to be sufficiently somber to enlist support around the world without creating panic here at home.

In 1961 he resisted the recommendation that he declare a full-scale national emergency over the threat to Berlin, recognizing that this resort to ultimate powers and public response had to be selectively used. For similar reasons, he has generally resisted urgings of disappointed partisans who would have him stir up the public against a Congress which is controlled (at least nominally) by his own party and which has consistently enacted four-fifths of his program.

In short, presidential appeals for public support must be at the right time and with the right frequency, if they are to be effective. On other occasions he may need to alienate a portion of his public support, for serving as President of all the people does not mean offending none of them. But this also cannot be done too often if he is to maintain his position, and it should not be done for meaningless or hopeless causes. President Kennedy may have struck the right balance, for

47

he is criticized, on the one hand, for expanding the powers of his office, sending too much to the Congress, and taking on too many controversies, and, at the same time, for "hoarding" his popularity and recognizing the limitations of a largely lethargic electorate.

One important distinction should be kept in mind. In domestic affairs, a presidential decision is usually the beginning of public debate. In foreign affairs, the issues are frequently so complex, the facts so obscure, and the period for decision so short, that the American people have from the beginning—and even more so in this century—delegated to the President more discretion in this vital area; and they are usually willing to support any reasonable decision he makes.

But public opinion cannot be taken for granted. Some Presidents have tried to change it, others have rushed to catch up with it, but none has repeatedly defied it. "With public sentiment on its side," Lincoln said with some exaggeration, "everything succeeds; with public sentiment against it, nothing succeeds." Franklin D. Roosevelt wrote: "I cannot go any faster than the people will let me." And President Kennedy is acutely aware of Jefferson's dictum: "Great innovations should not be forced on slender majorities."

President Kennedy, for example, has pressed a divided Congress and a contented public to abandon century-old economic precepts and accept a sizable tax cut with a sizable deficit at a time of general prosperity, but, unwilling to be so far out in front of Congress and the country that his program would have no chance, he stretched out the proposed tax cut to avoid a peacetime deficit larger than that of his predecessor.

No President respects public opinion simply out of fear of impeachment or even solely out of a desire for reelection—for the same principle is followed in both his terms. Instead both his conscience and his common sense, both his principles and his political judgment, compel him to seek, to the extent possible, the approval of the voters who elected him and who can defeat his party, the consent of the governed who are affected by his decision and on whose consent its success may depend.

Every President must, therefore, be a keen judge of public opinion. He must be able to distinguish its petty whims, to estimate its endurance, to respond to its impatience, and to respect its potential power. He must know how best and how often he can appeal to the public—and when it is better left undisturbed.

No President reaches that summit of public favor without believing he possesses (and he usually does) an extraordinary instinct for public opinion. He does not rely on the views expressed in his mail, or in public petitions, or by pickets in front of the White House, for they all too often reflect only a tiny organized group. He does not rely on opinion polls, which, outside of testing comparative candidate strengths, are still an inexact measure of the voters' views. He does not rely on the crowds that greet him on his travels, knowing they are usually a disproportionately partisan sample. Nor does he generalize from conversations with visitors, reports from his advisers, or his reading and viewing of mass media. His political intuition is in part an amalgamation of all of these—but he is likely to regard his own invisible antennae as somehow more sensitive than any. (President McKinley, according to Speaker Cannon, retained his popularity by "keeping his ear so close to the ground he got it full of grasshoppers.")

I no longer believe those who say that a poor politician could be a good President, "if he could only be appointed to the job." Without the qualities required of a successful candidate—without the ability to rally support, to understand the public, to express its aspirations—without the organizational talent, the personal charm, and the physical stamina required to survive the primaries, the convention, and the election—no man would make a great President, however wise in other ways he might be.

PRESSURE GROUPS, CONGRESS, AND THE PRESS

Each President must also judge when to oppose or accommodate a single segment of public opinion—a region or state, an occupation or age group, an industry or profession, a pressure group or lobby. Some will have views the President respects, such as nuclear scientists on nuclear tests. Some will have influence he seeks to enlist, such as the organization of older citizens on behalf of his health bill. Some will have sufficient power to cause him concern, at least in their own sphere of influence. (The least respected and least effective lobbies in Washington, I might add, are those which rush forward to testify on every measure of every kind, whether directly related or not to the interests of their members. It is doubtful, for example, that President Roosevelt was either heartened or dismayed by the 1934 resolution of a bankers' organization stating that its members would stand solidly behind the President on all emergency measures that did not infringe on their interests.)

There will always be a small but noisy group of critics intolerant of the gap between hope and possibility, complaining of a lack of leadership when long-awaited measures are not immediately enacted, while an equally small and vocal group will wail that each step forward the President takes is a gross usurpation of power.

The amount of pressure generated by those concerned over import competition must be balanced against the less active but larger number of persons benefiting from both exports and imports. The political or congressional attacks induced by a contractor whose weapons system has been discontinued must be weighed against the long-range costs of continuing an outmoded system.

The task is not always one of choosing between two interests. No President, even if he so wished, could suspend the laws in response to complaints—with respect to desegregation or anti-trust, for example. But he may find it desirable to accept amendments to a tax measure, or to reach informal understandings on concessions regarding a trade bill, in order to secure the passage of those bills with the support of a diverse coalition; or he may warn his appointees against exhibiting an attitude toward business or labor that is so hostile it might dampen the economic climate.

A President's own ties with some economic or other interest group may give him additional bargaining power with that group or reduced influence with another. A President with close ties to business, for example, will meet less resistance to his anti-inflation or anti-trust efforts. On the other hand, while it should not be impossible to find an equitable constitutional formula to settle the church-school aid problem, it is difficult for that formula to be suggested by the nation's first Catholic President.

Pressure groups usually have less direct effect on the President than on his relations with the Congress—a large and separate topic but a major arena of presidential politics. While this discussion is concerned primarily with White House decisions, members of the

Congress will inevitably attempt to affect those decisions in much the same way as the White House attempts to affect the decisions of the Congress: i.e., legislators will privately or publicly lobby, pressure, encourage, or discourage the President and his advisers, with respect to his legislative program or budget, both before and after their passage through the Congress.

As is true of public opinion and segments thereof, the views of one or more members of Congress must sometimes be resisted, sometimes reshaped, sometimes ignored, and sometimes accepted, depending not only on the validity of those views but on the power of those who express them and on the extent to which they are shared throughout the Congress. Presidents have differed in the degree of their deference to (or domination of) congressional opinion, according to their own legislative experience, their control of their party, and their party's control of the Congress, but all Presidents since Washington have noted the change in climate that occurs when Congress adjourns.

Finally, presidential politics includes attention to the American press and other media. Their selection and description of particular events—far more than their editorials—help to create or promote national issues, to shape the minds of the Congress and public, and to influence the President's agenda and timing. Ever since George Washington expressed the wish in 1777 "that our Printers were more discreet in many of their publications," our Presidents and the press have engaged in what the jargon of the Cold War would call a "contest for men's minds."

The winning side in this contest is debatable. The advent of television has given the President great resources for directly reaching the public, but even presidential corrections rarely catch up with those misstatements which now and then appear in the press. For example, the great newspaper chain which headlined a totally false scare story about Soviet planes overflying the southeastern United States has never acknowledged its error.

I have often been asked why President Kennedy, unlike his predecessor, should bother to read so many newspapers when so much of their important information and arguments—excluding overseas statements and events that occurred during the night—is at least twenty-four hours old to him. Obviously this would be even more true of weekly and monthly magazines. He reads them, I believe, partly to gain new insights for himself but primarily to know what the public and the Congress are reading, to see how his actions or choices appear to others without his access to the facts. For any President, any politician dependent on public opinion, is concerned with how that opinion is shaped, with how, to use a current phrase, the news is being "managed" in the only place it can be managed, the media editorial offices.

FIVE

Presidential Advisers

THE nation's press also serves (though not nearly to the extent it imagines) as a key presidential adviser, thus introducing my second major category, the only one of the three categories specifically mentioned in the Constitution. Article II, Section 2 provides that the President "may require the Opinion in writing of the principal Officer in each of the Executive Departments upon any subject relating to the Duties of their respective offices." But it does not prevent him from requiring their opinion *orally,* as the present incumbent frequently prefers in the early stages of decision. It does not prevent him from obtaining a Cabinet member's opinion on subjects *not* relating to his respective office—if a Secretary of Defense has a business background, for example, that would be helpful in a dispute with the steel industry—or if a Secretary of the

Treasury has experience in foreign affairs. Nor is the President prevented from seeking the opinions of those who are *not* principal officers of the Executive departments.

MEETING WITH ADVISERS

In short, each President must determine for himself how best to elicit and assess the advice of his advisers. Organized meetings, of the Cabinet and National Security Council, for example, have certain indispensable advantages, not the least of which are the increased public confidence inspired by order and regularity and the increased esprít de corps of the participants.

President Kennedy, whose nature and schedule would otherwise turn him away from meetings for the sake of meeting, has sometimes presided over sessions of the full Cabinet and National Security Council held primarily for these two reasons. Regularly scheduled meetings can also serve to keep open the channels of communication. This is the primary purpose, for example, of the President's weekly breakfast with his party's legislative leaders.

But there are other important advantages to meetings. The interaction of many minds is usually more illuminating than the intuition of one. In a meeting representing different departments and diverse points of view, there is a greater likelihood of hearing alternatives, of exposing errors, and of challenging assumptions. It is true in the White House, as in the Congress, that fewer votes are changed by open debate than by quiet negotiation among the debaters. But in the White House, unlike the Congress, only one man's vote is decisive, and thorough and thoughtful debate *before* he has made up his mind can assist him in that task.

That meetings can sometimes be useful was proven by the deliberations of the NSC executive committee after the discovery of offensive weapons in Cuba. The unprecedented nature of the Soviet move, the manner in which it cut across so many departmental jurisdictions, the limited amount of information available, and the security restrictions which inhibited staff work, all tended to have a leveling effect on the principals taking part in these discussions, so that each felt free to challenge the assumptions and assertions of all others.

Everyone in that group altered his views as the give-and-take talk continued. Every solution or combination of solutions was coldly examined, and its disadvantages weighed. The fact that we started out with a sharp divergence of views, the President has said, was "very valuable" in hammering out a policy.

In such meetings, a President must carefully weigh his own words. Should he hint too early in the proceedings at the direction of his own thought, the weight of his authority, the loyalty of his advisers and their desire to be on the "winning side" may shut off productive debate. Indeed, his very presence may inhibit candid discussion. President Truman, I am told, absented himself for this reason from some of the National Security Council discussions on the Berlin blockade; and President Kennedy, learning on his return from a mid-week trip in October, 1962, that the deliberations of the NSC executive committee over Cuba had been more spirited and frank in his absence, asked the committee to hold other preliminary sessions without him.

But no President—at least none with his firm cast of mind and concept of office—could stay out of the fray completely until all conflicts were resolved and a collective decision reached. For group recommendations too often put a premium on consensus in place of content, on unanimity in place of precision, on compromise in place of creativity.

Some advisers may genuinely mistake agreement for validity and coordination for policy—looking upon their own role as that of mediator, convinced that any conclusion shared by so many able minds must be right, and pleased that they could in this way ease their President's problems. They may in fact have increased them.

Even more severe limitations arise when a decision must be communicated, in a document or speech or diplomatic note. For group authorship is rarely, if ever, successful. A certain continuity and precision of style, and unity of argument, must be carefully drafted, particularly in a public communication that will be read or heard by many diverse audiences. Its key principles and phrases can be debated, outlined, and later reviewed by a committee, but basically authorship depends on one man alone with his typewriter or pen. (Had the Gettysburg address been written by a committee, its ten sentences would surely have grown to a hundred, its simple pledges would surely have been hedged, and the world would indeed have little noted or long remembered what was said there.)

Moreover, even spirited debates can be stifling as well as stimulating. The homely, the simple, or the safe may sound far more plausible to the weary ear in the Cabinet room than it would look to the careful eye in the office. The most formidable debater is not necessarily the most informed, and the most reticent may sometimes be the wisest.

Even the most distinguished and forthright adviser is usually reluctant to stand alone. If he fears his persistence in a meeting will earn him the disapprobation of his colleagues, a rebuff by the President, or (in case of a "leak") the outrage of the Congress, press, or public, he may quickly seek the safety of greater numbers. At the other extreme are those who seek refuge in the role of chronic dissenter, confining their analytical power to a restatement of dangers and objections.

Still others may address themselves more to their image than to the issues. The liberal may seek to impress his colleagues with his caution; idealists may try to sound tough-minded. I have attended more than one meeting where a military solution was opposed by military minds and supported by those generally known as peace-lovers.

The quality of White House meetings also varies with the number and identity of those attending. Large meetings are less likely to keep secrets—too many Washington officials enjoy talking knowingly at social events or to the press or to their friends. Large meetings are also a less flexible instrument for action, less likely to produce a meaningful consensus or a frank, hard-hitting debate. President Kennedy prefers to invite only those whose official views he requires or whose unofficial judgment he values, and to reserve crucial decisions for a still smaller session or for solitary contemplation in his own office.

The difficulty with small meetings, however, is that, in Washington, nearly everyone likes to feel that he, too, conferred and concurred. For years agencies and individuals all over town have felt affronted if not invited to a National Security Council session. The press leaps to conclusions as to who is in favor and who is not by scanning the attendance lists of meetings, speculating in much the same fashion (and with even less success) as the Kremlinologists who study the reviewing stand at the Russian May Day Parade or analyze which Soviet officials sat where at the opening of the Moscow ballet.

Yet in truth attendance at a White House meeting is not necessarily a matter of logic. Protocol, personal relations, and the nature of the forum may all affect the list. Some basic foreign policy issue, for example, may be largely decided before it comes to the National Security Council—by the appointment of a key official, or by the President's response at a press conference, or by the funds allocated in the budget. Yet personnel, press conference, and budget advice is generally given in meetings outside the National Security Council.

EXPERT ADVISERS

Many different types of advisers, with differing roles and contributions, attend these meetings. President Kennedy met on his tax policy in the summer of 1962, for example, with professional economists from both inside and outside the government, as well as with department heads and White House aides. To the key meetings on Cuba were invited highly respected Foreign Service officers as well as policy appointees, retired statesmen as well as personal presidential assistants.

There is no predictable weight which a President can give to the conclusions of each type. The technical expert or career specialist, operating below the policy-making level, may have concentrated knowledge on the issue under study which no other adviser can match. Yet Presidents are frequently criticized for ignoring the advice of their own experts.

The reason is that the very intensity of that expert's study may prevent him from seeing the broader, more practical perspective which must govern public policy. As Laski's notable essay pointed out, too many experts lack a sense of proportion, an ability to adapt, and a willingness to accept evidence inconsistent with their own. The specialist, Laski wrote, too often lacks "insight into the movement and temper of the public mind. . . . He is an invaluable servant and an impossible master."

Thus the atomic scientist, discussing new tests, may

think largely in terms of his own laboratory. The career diplomat, discussing an Asian revolt, may think largely in terms of his own post. The professional economist, in urging lower farm price supports, may think more in terms of his academic colleagues than of the next presidential election.

But not all experts recognize the limits of their political sagacity, and they do not hesitate to pronounce with a great air of authority broad policy recommendations in their own field (and sometimes all fields). Any President would be properly impressed by their seeming command of the complex; but the President's own common sense, his own understanding of the Congress and the country, his own balancing of priorities, his own ability to analyze and generalize and simplify, are more essential in reaching the right decision than all the specialized jargon and institutionalized traditions of the professional elite.

The trained navigator, it has been rightly said, is essential to the conduct of a voyage, but his judgment is not superior on such matters as where it should go or whether it should be taken at all. Essential to the relationship between expert and politician, therefore, is the recognition by each of the other's role, and the re-fusal of each to assume the other's role. The expert should neither substitute his political judgment for the policy-maker's nor resent the latter's exercising of his own; and the policy-maker should not forget which one is the expert.

Expert predictions are likely to be even more tenuous than expert policy judgments, particularly in an age when only the unpredictable seems to happen. In the summer of 1962, most of the top economists in govern-ment, business, and academic life thought it likely that a recession would follow the stock-market slide—at least "before the snows melted" was the cautious fore-cast by one economist from a cold northern state. But, instead, this year's thaw brought with it new levels of production—and, naturally, a new set of predictions.

In the fall of 1962, most specialists in Soviet affairs believed that long-range Soviet missiles, with their closely guarded electronic systems, would never be stationed on the uncertain island of Cuba, nearly 6,000 miles away from Soviet soil and supplies. Nevertheless, each rumor to this effect was checked out; increasing rumors brought increased surveillance; and when, finally, the unexpected did happen, this did not diminish the President's respect for these career servants. It merely demonstrated once again that the only infallible experts are those whose forecasts have never been tested.

CABINET ADVISERS

In short, a Cabinet of politicians and policy-makers is better than a Cabinet of experts. But a President will also weigh with care the advice of each Cabinet official. For the latter is also bound by inherent limitations. He was not necessarily selected for the President's confidence in his judgment alone—considerations of politics, geography, public esteem, and interest-group pressures may also have played a part, as well as his skill in administration.

Moreover, each department has its own clientele and point of view, its own experts and bureaucratic interests, its own relations with the Congress and certain subcommittees, its own statutory authority, objectives, and standards of success. No Cabinet member is free to ignore all this without impairing the morale and efficiency of his department, his standing therein, and his relations with the powerful interest groups and congressmen who consider it partly their own.

The President may ask for a Secretary's best judgment apart from the department's views, but in the mind of the average Secretary (and there have been many notable exceptions) the two may be hardly distinguishable. Whether he is the captive or the champion of those interests makes no practical difference. By reflecting in his advice to the President his agency's component bureaus, some of which he may not even control, he increases both his prestige within the department and his parochialism without.

Bureaucratic parochialism and rivalry are usually associated in Washington with the armed services, but they in fact affect the outlook of nearly every agency. They can be observed, to cite only a few examples, in the jurisdictional maneuvering between the Park Service and the Forest Service, between the Bureau of Reclamation and the Army Engineers, between State and Treasury on world finance, or State and Commerce on world trade, or State and Defense on world disarmament.

They can also be observed in Cabinet autobiographies complaining that the President—any President—rarely saw things their way. And they can be observed, finally, in case studies of an agency head paying more heed to the Congress than to the President who named him. But it is the Congress, after all, that must pass on his requests for money, men, and authority. It is the Congress with which much of his time will be spent, which has the power to investigate his acts or alter his duties. And it is the Congress which vested many of his responsibilities directly in him, not in the President or the Executive branch.

WHITE HOUSE STAFF ADVISERS

The parochialism of experts and department heads is offset in part by a President's White House and executive staff. These few assistants are the only other men in Washington whose responsibilities both enable and require them to look, as he does, at the government as a whole. Even the White House specialists— the President's economic advisers or science adviser, for example—are likely to see problems in a broader perspective, within the framework of the President's objectives and without the constraints of bureaucratic tradition.

White House staff members are chosen, not according to any geographical, political, or other pattern, but for their ability to serve the President's needs and to talk the President's language. They must not—and do not, in this Administration—replace the role of a Cabinet official or block his access to the President. Instead, by working closely with departmental personnel, by spotting, refining, and defining issues for the President, they can increase governmental unity rather than splinter responsibility. A good White House staff can give a President that crucial margin of time, analysis, and judgment that makes an unmanageable problem more manageable.

But there are limiting factors as well. A White House adviser may see a departmental problem in a wider context than the Secretary, but he also has less contact with actual operations and pressures, with the Congress and interested groups. If his own staff grows too large, his office may become only another department, another level of clearances and concurrences instead of a personal instrument of the President. If his confidential relationship with the President causes either one to be too uncritical of the other's judgment, errors may go uncorrected. If he develops (as Mr. Acheson has suggested so many do) a confidence in his own competence which outruns the fact, his contribution may be more mischievous than useful. If, on the other hand, he defers too readily to the authority of renowned experts and Cabinet powers, then the President is denied the skeptical, critical service his staff should be providing.

OUTSIDE ADVISERS

Finally, a President may seek or receive advice from outside the Executive branch: from members of the Congress; from independent wise men, elder statesmen, academic lights; from presidentially named high-level commissions or special agents; or merely from conversations with friends, visitors, private interest leaders, and others. Inevitably, unsolicited advice will pour in from the mass media.

This is good. Every President needs independent, unofficial sources of advice for the same reasons he needs independent, unofficial sources of information. Outside advisers may be more objective. Their contact with affected groups may be closer. They may be men whose counsel the President trusts, but who are unable to accept government service for financial or personal reasons. They may be men who are frank with the President because, to use Corwin's phrase, their "daily political salt did not come from the President's table."

Whatever the justification, outside advice has its own limitations. As national problems become more complex and interrelated, requiring continuous, firsthand knowledge of confidential data and expert analysis, very few outsiders are sufficiently well informed. The fact that some simple recommendation, contained in an editorial or political oration or informal conversation, seems more striking or appealing or attention-getting than the intricate product of bureaucracy does not make it any more valid.

Moreover, once the advice of a distinguished private citizen or committee is sought and made public, rejection of that advice may add to the President's difficulties. The appointment by the last three Presidents of special advisory committees on civil rights, world trade, and foreign aid was, in that sense, a gamble—a gamble that the final views of these committees would strengthen, not weaken, the President's purpose. Should the outside report not be made public, the Gaither report being a well-known example, a President who rejects its advice may still have to face the consequences of its authors' displeasure.

QUALIFICATIONS OF ADVISERS

Finally, a President's evaluation of any individual's advice is dependent in part on the human characteristics of both men. Personalities play an intangible but surprisingly important role. Particular traits, social ties, recreational interests or occupational backgrounds may strengthen or weaken the bonds between them. Some Presidents pay more attention to generals, some to businessmen, some to politicians, some even to intellectuals who have "never met a payroll and never carried a precinct."

In truth, a political background, not necessarily at the precinct level, is helpful. It gives the adviser a more realistic understanding of the President's needs. Those without such experience will tend to assume that the few congressmen in touch with their agency speak for

74

all the Congress, that one or two contacts at a Washington cocktail party are an index of public opinion, and that what looms large in the newspaper headlines necessarily looms large in the public mind.

Those with a political base of their own are also more secure in case of attack; but those with political ambitions of their own—as previous Presidents discovered—may place their own reputation and record ahead of their President's. (Such a man is not necessarily suppressing his conscience and forgetting the national interest. He may sincerely believe whatever it is most to his advantage to believe, much like the idealistic but hungry lawyer who will never defend a guilty man but persuades himself that all rich clients are innocent.)

Other advisers may also be making a record, not for some future campaign, but for some future publication. "History will record that I am right," he mutters to himself, if not to his colleagues, because he intends to write that history in his memoirs. The inaccuracy of most Washington diaries and autobiographies is surpassed only by the immodesty of their authors.

The opposite extreme is the adviser who tells his President only what he thinks the President wants to hear—a bearer of consistently good tidings but frequently bad advice.

Yet there is no sure test of a good adviser. The most rational, pragmatic-appearing man may turn out to be the slave of his own private myths, habits, and emotional beliefs. The hardest-working man may be too busy and out-of-touch with the issue at hand, or too weary to focus firmly on it. (I saw first-hand, during the long days and nights of the Cuban crisis, how brutally physical and mental fatigue can numb the good sense as well as the senses of normally articulate men.)

The most experienced man may be experienced only in failure, or his experience, in Coleridge's words, may be "like the stern lights of a ship which illumine only the track it has passed." The most articulate, authoritative man may only be making bad advice sound good, while driving into silence less aggressive or more cautious advisers.

All this a President must weigh in hearing his advisers. He need not weigh them equally. For toward some, he will have more respect. With some, he will communicate easier. For some, he will have more affection.

President Kennedy's confidence in the Attorney General, for example, on a wide variety of issues, is based not on fraternal ties alone but on long years of observing and testing his brother's judgment and dependability. The more active role taken by Secretary of Labor Goldberg, also assumed by his successor but in contrast with that of his predecessors, resulted not from an upgrading of that post but from a closer relationship with the President.

There are countless other examples. My emphasis on the role of the President has not made me a turncoat to the distinguished class of presidential advisers. On the contrary, while his perspective may be more limited, the career specialist, the Cabinet Secretary, the White House aide, or any other adviser still has a valuable contribution to make; and his limited perspective is a danger only if both he and the President are blind to that limitation.

SIX

The Presidential Perspective

BUT advisers, however respected, are still advisers; and the Constitutional Convention, after long debate as to whether the President should, in effect, be required to accept the views of his Executive Council, instead entrusted the final power of decision to the one man with the most comprehensive perspective—the President. That unique perspective is the third and final ingredient to be blended in this mix.

The authors of the presidential office made it clear that they were not adopting the British Cabinet system. Hamilton thought it would be "a clog upon a President's good intentions . . . and a cloak to conceal his faults." Every President, to be sure, will always consult with his senior officials and respect their views. It may be that he will "rarely fail . . . to accept their recommendations," as Coolidge claimed in his case; or it may be that he will "make all of his own decisions," as Ickes' diary complained about Roosevelt. The important fact is that the choice is his.

OVERRULING HIS ADVISERS

It is not a choice to be exercised lightly. In choosing between conflicting advice, the President is also choosing between conflicting advisers, conferring recognition on some while rebuffing others. He will, consequently, take care to pay more attention to the advice of the man who must carry out the decision than the advice of a mere "kibitzer." He will be slow to overrule a Cabinet officer whose pride or prestige have been committed, not only to ease that officer's personal feelings but to maintain his utility and credibility.

He will also go far to accept the advice of a man whose public image is helpful to his policy; and in this sense, decisions are partially made whenever the President selects an appointee with a known position and reputation. Indeed, all appointees have both prerogatives and responsibilities which a President must recognize in the interests of good relations. President Kennedy, for example, has, on more than one occasion, taken pains to make it clear that the Secretary of State is his principal adviser in foreign affairs—thereby building up the morale, the enthusiasm, and the competence of the Department of State while backing up the Secretary's own authority and prestige.

Whenever any President overrules any Secretary, he runs the risk of that Secretary grumbling, privately, if not publicly, to the Congress or to the press (or to his diary), or dragging his feet on implementation, or, at the very worst, resigning with a blast at the President. It is rare, of course, for any appointee leaving office to have more public appeal than a President in office. The whirlpools he expects to stir up with his dramatic resignation and published exposés are soon lost in a tide of other events over which the President continues to ride.

Nevertheless, the violent resignation of almost any Secretary of State, Secretary of Defense, or Secretary of the Treasury could cause his chief considerable trouble; and other appointees could cause trouble in their own circles. Neustadt reports that Truman did not want his position on a steel settlement undermined by a public protest or resignation from Secretary of Commerce Sawyer. Rosenman commented that Roosevelt could not afford politically to alienate Cordell Hull to the point of resignation. Wilson was fearful—mistakenly, it turned out—that the blame would be placed on him when Bryan resigned from the Cabinet. And, though no resignations were even potentially involved, the fact that a majority of all the responsible officials in the Cuban crisis "came to accept the course we finally took," President Kennedy has said, "made it much easier."

(Even Hamilton, the first champion of the strong Presidency, while restating that "a President is not bound to conform to the advice of his ministers," nevertheless agreed that "the Constitution presumes he will consult them . . . it must be his own fault if he be not surrounded by men who, for ability and integrity, deserve his confidence. And if his ministers are of this character, the consulting of them will always be likely to be useful.")

In short, almost every President is as reluctant to overrule the determined opposition of his advisers as he is to veto an act of the Congress. He rules, to a degree, not only with their advice but with their consent.

But this is true only to a degree. Consultation is not slavish adherence, and consent may often be induced. For only one man under our system is President. Only one man bears all the burdens of responsibility. Only one man, with his running-mate, is accountable to all the people.

Advisers may delay their advice, change their minds, and offer several alternatives. But their roles and responsibilities are wholly different from his. Their views and visions of where the world is moving are far less grand than his. "No matter how many advisers you have," as President Kennedy said on television, "the President must finally choose. . . . [He] bears the burden . . . the advisers may move on to new advice."

Jefferson, Jackson, Lincoln, Theodore Roosevelt, Wilson, Franklin D. Roosevelt—all judged to be "strong" Presidents—declined to use the Cabinet as a voting board of directors. "I have gathered you together," Lincoln told his Cabinet regarding the Emancipation Proclamation, "to hear what I have written down. I do not wish your advice about the main matter—that I have determined for myself."

Similarly, Jackson declared: "I have accustomed myself to receive with respect the opinions of others, but always take the responsibility of deciding for myself." Theodore Roosevelt said: "In a crisis, the duty of a leader is to lead—and not to take refuge behind the generally timid wisdom of a multitude of counsellors." And Wilson summed up the presidential perspective best of all. "I cannot choose as an individual what I shall do," he said; "I must choose always as a President, ready to guard at every turn and in every way possible the success of what I have to do for the people."

PRESIDENTIAL SELF-ASSERTION

Some may think that statement immodest. But a President cannot afford to be modest. No one else sits where he sits or knows all that he knows. No one else has his power to lead, to inspire, or to restrain the Congress and country. If he fails to lead, no one leads. "The buck," in Truman's words, "stops here."

A President knows that his name will be the label for a whole era. Textbooks yet unwritten and schoolchildren yet unborn will hold him responsible for all that happens. His program, his power, his prestige, his place in history, perhaps his reelection, will all be affected by key decisions. His appointees, however distinguished they may be in their own right, will rise or fall as he rises or falls. Even his White House aides, who see him constantly, cannot fully perceive his personal stakes and isolation. And no amount of tinkering with the presidential machinery, or establishment of new executive offices, can give anyone else *his* perspective.

Consequently, self-confidence and self-assertion are more important than modesty. The nation selects its President, at least in part, for his philosophy and his judgment and his conscientious conviction of what is right—and he need not hesitate to apply them. He must believe in his own objectives. He must assert his own priorities. And he must strive always to preserve the power and prestige of his office, the availability of his options, and the long-range interests of the nation.

To illustrate: If the good faith and prestige of his office have been engaged in an effort to achieve a steel wage settlement which would make any price increase unnecessary, then such an increase, announced immediately after that settlement is reached, requires a different kind of response than might otherwise have been necessary.

Economists may tell him that devaluation of the dollar would be the quickest and cheapest solution to our balance of payments and gold flow deficits. But as chief custodian of the national honor—mindful of the effect such a move would have on our international role and prestige, and on the confidence of other nations for decades to come—he prefers to chip away at the deficit by slower, more painful methods.

A member of the Congress or the press can achieve some measure of fame by reporting rumors or stating problems or raising questions. But that is not enough for a President. Refugee reports of offensive Soviet missiles installed on the island of Cuba, for example, recurred for well over a year before such missiles were actually brought in. Each report was methodically checked out by intelligence authorities; and so long as their findings were negative, no President—whatever others were saying—could stake the dignity of his office and the security of the nation on unfounded rumors and exaggeration. And once such a threat was found to exist it was preferable to adopt a course which, as President Kennedy has described it, "had the advantage of permitting other steps if this one was unsuccessful."

A President who asserts the presidential perspective and disturbs the status quo will always engender criticism. As a result of his involving his office, either directly or through his staff, in many problems at early stages, he is accused, in effect, of presidential interference with the Executive branch (which is true). As a result of his taking the initiative in a troubled world and on a cluttered agenda, he is accused of adjusting the powers of his office to the needs of his time (which is also true). And, finally, as a result of his staking the prestige of his office on all kinds of matters affecting the public good, he is accused of taking unto himself the right to define as well as defend the national interest (and this also is true).

For Woodrow Wilson summed up the President's role in his lectures at Columbia: "No one else represents the people as a whole. . . . His is the only voice in national affairs . . . representative . . . of the whole people." And President Kennedy, when a Senator and candidate, declared: "Upon him alone converge all the needs and aspirations of all parts of the country, all departments of the government, all nations of the world."

SEVEN

By Way of Summary

I CAN only offer a conclusion which all of us already know: that the only way to assure good presidential decisions is to elect and support good Presidents. For in mixing all these ingredients, his style and standard, his values and vitality, his insights and outlook will make the crucial difference. A great presidential decision defies the laws of mathematics and exceeds the sum of all its parts. A great President is not the product of his staff but the master of his house.

He must know when to reject the advice of his experts and when to back up a Secretary. He must be able to win a consensus without waiting for one. He must be attuned to public opinion but not bound by it. He must know the limitations of his office as well as its powers. He must reign in Washington, but he must also rule.

That is the kind of Presidency in which I believe; that is the kind of President I believe we now have; and that is the kind of President I believe we must always have.

Unlike the leaders of autocracy, the President of our democracy must contend with powerful pressures of public opinion, with co-equal branches of the government, and with a free and critical press. He cannot allocate resources, or ignore traditions, or override departments in whatever manner he wishes. His allies cannot be treated as satellites, his mistakes cannot be concealed, his critics cannot be silenced.

But over the long haul, democratic decision-making, for all its faults and failures, will, I believe, produce superior decisions. True, a totalitarian leader can exercise absolute command over his advisers and absolute compulsion over ideology. But he cannot command good advice and he cannot compel new ideas. Suppression and terror may suffice for the efficient control of machinery, but they cannot improve the decisions of men.

For great and lasting decisions in human affairs can only be made by those exposed to human value judgments. Consistently wise decisions can only be made by those whose wisdom is constantly challenged. The voluntary unity of free men and nations is ultimately more solid than the forced uniformity of repression. In the long run, there can be no wisdom without dissent, no progress without diversity, no greatness without responsibility.

Whatever party or person is in the White House, these basic truths will prevail. For in our political system, as we learned long ago in our religion, "there are diversities of gifts but the same Spirit. And there are differences of administrations, but the same Lord."

Index